The Inside-Out BEAUTY BOOK

Books by
Sandra Byrd
FROM BETHANY HOUSE PUBLISHERS

Girl Talk
A Growing-Up Guide
The Inside-Out Beauty Book
Stuff 2 Do

THE HIDDEN DIARY
Cross My Heart
Make a Wish
Just Between Friends
Take a Bow
Pass It On
Change of Heart
Take a Chance
One Plus One

GIRLS ♥ LIKE YOU!

The Inside-Out BEAUTY BOOK

Tips & Tools for Girls Like You

Sandra Byrd

BETHANYHOUSE
Minneapolis, Minnesota

Published by Bethany House Publishers
11400 Hampshire Avenue South
Bloomington, Minnesota 55438
www.bethanyhouse.com

Bethany House Publishers is a Division of
Baker Book House Company, Grand Rapids, Michigan.

Printed in the United States of America

Library of Congress Cataloging-in-Publication Data

Byrd, Sandra.
    The inside-out beauty book : tips and tools for girls like you / by Sandra Byrd.
        v.   cm.
    ISBN 0-7642-2493-X
    1. Grooming for girls—Juvenile literature.   2. Girls—Health and hygiene—Juvenile literature.   [1. Beauty, Personal.   2. Grooming.   3. Health. 4. Christian life.]   I.Title.
    RA777.25   .B97   2002
    646.7'046—dc21   2002002712

I remember the day I bought my first bottle of Love's Baby Soft perfume. The bottle was pretty and pink, and I gave the cashier my own money before she carefully wrapped my purchase. Each morning before school I'd spray the tiniest amount on my neck and on my wrist, under my watch. I was old enough to wear something light and pretty, and I was becoming more a young lady and less a little girl.

This book is dedicated with love to all the young ladies just discovering the beauty God has lovingly bestowed on them, inside and out.

Contents

SANDRA BYRD lives near beautiful Seattle, between the snow-capped Mount Rainier and the Space Needle, with her husband and two children (and let's not forget her golden retriever, Duchess). When she's not writing, she's usually reading, but she also likes to scrapbook, listen to music, and spend time with friends. Besides writing *The Inside-Out Beauty Book*, she's also the author of THE HIDDEN DIARY books and the bestselling series SECRET SISTERS.

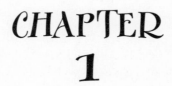

CHAPTER
1

More Than a Mirror

Mirror, mirror, hanging there,
Who's the prettiest, the most fair?

—Snow White

Have you ever been to a carnival where there was a wavy mirror? When you move around, it makes you look shorter/taller/fatter/thinner than you really are. The closer you get, the more smashed together you look! From farther away, you look stretched out. Looking into a "regular" mirror is something we do five or ten times a day. We check our hair before we go to school or check our braces after eating. But even a "normal" mirror can't show the whole truth.

A mirror is just a piece of glass with a thin layer of silver or aluminum stuck on it. It only reflects what is on the outside. It can't see into your soul or your mind or your heart—the most important parts of the real you. The most important parts of you will always shine through—love, grace, gentleness, and humor—no matter what you look like on the outside.

Get a silver or stainless steel soup spoon out of the kitchen drawer. Look at your reflection on the back of the spoon— the curvy part. Now slowly move your face to the left, then to the right. Like what you see? Ha! Chipmunk cheeks, right? Now flip the spoon over and look at your reflection on the inside, too. What happened? You're upside-down and all stretched out. Now stick your tongue out! Reflections aren't always trustworthy, are they?

Is it bad if we care about our outer beauty?

You might be surprised by the answer: No!

The book of James implies that looking into a mirror but doing nothing to correct your appearance, if it needs it, is silly. The Bible talks about Ruth taking a bath, perfuming herself, and putting on nice clothes when she wanted to make a good impression. Christians are the temple of the Holy Spirit and should take good care of themselves. Are you making the most of what God has given you, being pleased with what you have? Or are you always wishing for something else?

Ruth was concerned with her outer self. But her inner beauty—her loyalty, her love, and her faithfulness—was what made her lovely and what we remember her for. In fact, today no one knows what she looked like, but everyone knows her heart. Just work for the right balance between thinking about the outer you and the inner you and you'll be fine.

Growth Chart

From the day you are born, doctors check to see that you are growing at a healthy pace. This works for your inner self, too. Like it was for Ruth, our main source of beauty should be inside. We don't spend much time checking on that, but it's very important.

Are you growing up inside, too? You can make a chart at home that measures your spiritual health. On a scale of one to ten, rate yourself on these things:

Love:
Joy:
Peace:
Patience:
Kindness:
Goodness:
Faithfulness:
Gentleness:
Self-control:
    (See Galatians 5:22)

How can you grow more in each of these areas? Each day, turn more of your life over to the control of the Holy Spirit. You will be healthier—and more beautiful—inside and out.

Do you think boys look at inner beauty or only outer beauty?

Overheard: Some boys were having a conversation about girls. They mentioned one girl being pretty. But they also talked about another girl having a laugh that made them want to smile (reflecting her joy). Then they compared two others—one who freaked out when she got a bad grade on a report and one girl who handled disappointment well (reflecting her self-control).

There's no doubt that *all* of us consider what someone looks like on the outside—at first. But when we *really* like someone, we are attracted to what is on the inside. Boys are probably interested in both. Some boys are most attracted by what a person looks like.

Other boys are more interested in a person's inner beauty—her joy, her sense of humor, her kindness, her curiosity. What kind of boy do you want to like you—one who looks more at the outside or what's on the inside?

If your spirit is beautiful, will you be beautiful on the outside, too?

Yes. People will want to be with you—and they may not even know why! What's on the inside always shows on the outside—whether it is good or bad.

> ### As a face is reflected in water, so the heart reflects the person.
> Proverbs 27:19

"I Wish I Looked Like Jenna"

Once you get a bit older, you become aware of how other people around you look. Ever notice how some of your friends have what you wish you did? They have pretty brown hair, while yours is blond. Or maybe they have dimples, while you have freckles.

It never seems just right. As long as you compare yourself to others, it never *will* be just right. In fact . . .

There are foot and hand models, eyebrow models, and lip models! They are people whose "parts" are more beautiful than other people's, but the rest of their bodies are just like everyone else's.

We don't live in a magazine world, though. We can't take pieces of one person and add them to pieces of another person and come out with a perfect look. Each girl has something that is especially nice, whether it is her eyes or her hands or her hair. But we also all have mostly average parts. We are unique.

As long as you compare yourself to the prettiest girls to see if you are good enough, you will be unhappy. Instead, compliment that person on her smile or her clothes, but be quietly pleased that you love your eye color and your pretty nails.

The secret of happiness is to be satisfied with who you are. You really are beautiful to God and to others.

> *You made my whole being. You formed me in my mother's body. I praise you because you made me in an amazing and wonderful way. What you have done is wonderful. I know this very well.*
>
> ❀ Psalm 139:13–14 (ICB)

Did You Know?

Police and crime labs use fingerprints and palm prints to positively identify a person. There are no two people in the world with the same fingerprints.

This isn't only true with fingerprints, you know. No one can copy you—and you can't really copy anyone else. You are free to be yourself.

You Asked

Does God like the beauty inside our hearts?

Yes. Here it is in His own words. . . .

> *God does not see the same way people see. People look at the outside of a person, but the Lord looks at the heart.*

> ❀ 1 Samuel 16:7b (ICB)

Most of the time you try to clean your fingerprints *off* of windows and mirrors, but this time, you're going to put some *on*!

Place your thumb up against the mirror you normally use to get ready. Can you see your print? You've got a one-in-the-world print!

If your print doesn't come out dark enough to see, cut a piece of paper into a one-inch square. Make a thumbprint by pressing your thumb down on a small pad of ink and then onto the paper square. You can use cool colors from the craft store—frosty green, hot blue. If you don't have an ink pad, you can take a marker and color it over your thumb. Tape the thumbprint to your mirror.

Each time you're getting ready, look at your thumbprint and remind yourself that you are the only *you* in the world, and no one will have just your look, just your tastes, or just your personal style.

Meet Leah . . .
A Girl Like You

Leah has always been very short, a dwarf. In fact, when people see her, the first thing they always notice is how different she is from everyone else. That can be hard to deal with, and it can be hard to get people to see the "real" you when you're very different on the outside. Leah, as you'll see, has a faith and quiet spirit that shine strongly, setting an example for others. Once you know her, you see that is her real difference and the source of her real beauty. Here's her story, in her own words:

I am a little person, a dwarf, or a person of short stature. The word *midget* is often hurtful, so it's better to use those other words.

When did you realize that you are built differently from most other girls?

When I was around three I went to Sunday school and learned that God made all living things grow. I asked my mom, if God made all living things grow, why was I not going to grow as tall as everyone else? Her response was that I was special!

As far as people making fun of me, there have been many. But the one that I think has affected me the most was a grown man who looked at me and just laughed and kept laughing. I kept a smile on my face, but you better believe the second I got in the car I cried. It was a point in my life when I decided that, no matter what other people thought of my body, I was going to have to accept it, because in life you can't take your body back with a receipt. I began to learn that the more I accepted myself, the more others did, too!

What kinds of trouble do little people have as kids?

I wanted to do the same things they were doing, but I oftentimes was left in the dust as they ran off because I couldn't run as fast as they did! I remember being in the second grade, and at recess every day all the girls would race each other across the monkey bars. My arms were too short to reach from monkey bar to monkey bar. But I will never forget a couple of years later. When most girls were finished climbing the monkey bars, I crossed them for the first time and couldn't have been more excited!

What would you say to other kids who are worried about how they look?

One of my favorite things in the world to do is pottery. If my pottery could talk and were to tell me that it didn't like the color I had painted it or that it was too big of a bowl it would make me sad. It didn't realize that I had made it big so it could hold a lot of fruit, and that I had made it the color it was to stand out so that people would notice it first! I made that bowl for a reason and a purpose. It's the same with God. He made us for a reason and a purpose, and the more we accept the way we are, the more we can realize our true potential.

There is a surgery out now that lengthens bones. I have the choice of lengthening my bones if I want to become tall, but that would go directly opposite of what I was made for. Why go against the thing that God gave me and only me? It was no mistake that I'm little. He made me for a purpose in this world.

I really feel that if you can accept the person that you are as you are, then it automatically shines on the outside as beauty! But don't worry—I still paint my toenails and give myself facials just to pamper this beautiful body that I'm in!

Leah's learned that no matter what you look like, you are uniquely you. God thought about you before you were made, and He made you—knitted you together, as the Bible says. Everyone has strong points and weak points—we are not just parts, but a whole person. The same genes that gave you great hair may also have given you oily skin. What is up to you, though, is your inner beauty—your heart, your actions, your attitude, and your spiritual life. It is how we grow in those things, as well as how we appreciate and accept what we look like, that shapes our true beauty. Peace, faith, and contentment glow from the inside out. Be someone who loves herself, not in a conceited way but in a thankful way, and watch how it draws people to you and how wonderful and warm you feel inside.

CHAPTER 2

Skin Deep

*She was so very beautiful, and fainting
had not changed her lovely skin at all.*

—Sleeping Beauty

Did you know that your skin is the largest organ your body has? It's mainly there to protect you and hold you together. It stops liquids like water and blood from escaping the inside of your body. It also stops many bacteria, chemicals, and dirt from entering your body, thereby preventing sickness. Your skin protects you from the sun.

Just like a big country that might have a desert, a mountain range, and an ocean shore within its territory, your skin covers a lot of area and has different needs. The biggest need all skin has is to be kept clean and protected. We are like that on the inside, too, aren't we? The Lord tells us if we confess our sins and repent, He will clean us on the inside. And He says He will go before us, stay with us, and never leave us or forget us. Now, that's *real* protection!

Let's find out what our skin does.

By sweating, your skin helps keep your body temperature normal. Glands in your skin release sweat when you get too hot. The sweat evaporates, and that cools down your body. You can sweat, on average, a couple of cups of water each day. That's about as much as can be held in an olive jar! (Sometimes it smells like vinegar, too!) Sweat isn't just sticky and smelly. It's healthy! Besides sweat on your skin, some bacteria live there, too. In fact, there are tens of thousands—if not more—of bacteria per square inch of your skin. Just think of that next time you lick your fingers. Eewww!

Why does it smell when you sweat?

When you sweat, the water interacts with the bacteria on your skin. Sometimes the bacteria themselves just have an odor—for example, the bacteria under your armpits. That's why there are antiperspirants, which control the perspiration or sweat, and deodorants, which control the odor from your glands. If you are sweating under your armpits but there's no odor, just use an antiperspirant. If there is an odor but not too much sweat, just use a deodorant. If odor *and* sweat are there, use something that has both an antiperspirant and a deodorant. A quick read of the label will tell you which products do what. The reason you *can* sweat is because your skin is actually seventy percent water!

Water, Water Everywhere

What you eat definitely affects your skin. Your skin needs lots of vitamin C, which is found in fruits such as oranges, lemons, and strawberries. It also needs vitamin E, found in whole grain breads and oatmeal. Most important, because your body is mostly water, you need to drink a lot of water to keep your skin soft and smooth. Eight small glasses—about eight ounces each—of water every day is best (pop and sugary sports drinks don't count). Water can't be stored in your body for long; it has to be drunk every day. In fact, your body can live much longer without food than without water.

Living Water

Why do we have to drink water every single day? Because what we drink is used up each day. Your body can live for a long time without food, but only a few days without water. In the same way, your soul needs "water" to live, too. Jesus provides the water that is necessary for spiritual life. This isn't water from a well or a faucet. Jesus calls it "living water"—water that gives eternal life. Once you have His life in you, you can be satisfied, because He gives spiritual life that springs up inside of you forever, day by day. You have a new life, a life you give to Him once for eternity. It's a decision you must choose to live out each day. When you live this way, you feel good, and you *are* good, inside and out.

> *[Jesus said,] "But whoever drinks the water I give will never be thirsty again. The water I give will become a spring of water flowing inside him. It will give him eternal life."*
>
> John 4:14 (ICB)

If you drink enough water, you can have smooth, healthy skin, but what will make you truly beautiful is remembering each day that you have Christ inside. Make choices based on His gift of eternal life and constant help right now. From now on, each time you drink from a water fountain (spring of water) at school, church, or the mall, take a moment to thank Jesus for His tender love and the living water and eternal life He provided for you.

The Nerve!

Our skin has a lot more to it than the pores that let the sweat out. It also has lots of nerve receptors in it. These help us tell if something is hot or cold or if something is painful. The nerve endings help to protect us. Think what would happen if you rested your hand on a red-hot stove burner if you couldn't feel heat or pain! God also lets us feel pleasure through these nerve receptors. Think of the gentle brush of a feather on your arm, someone scratching your back, or a self-given foot massage.

It is almost impossible to tickle yourself. Your brain already knows it's just you. Try it!

Why do people have different skin colors?

There are hundreds of unique skin colors. If you look even in the same family, brothers and sisters often have different shades of skin. The color of a person's skin depends mainly on the amount of a brown pigment—kind of like a dye—called melanin, produced in the skin. Dark-skinned people make more melanin than light-skinned people do. Mainly the genes you get from your mom and dad determine the amount of melanin produced in your skin.

Freckles are small spots of melanin. Being in the sun can increase melanin. This is what happens when you get a tan.

Is getting a tan bad?

Yes. Sorry to break the bad news. Tanning—and burning—can lead to skin cancer. Skin cancer starts in the cells of your skin, but some kinds can spread throughout your whole body. It can take a long time to develop, so if you get a sunburn this year, it could lead to cancer twenty years from now! One estimate says that people will be exposed to eighty percent of their lifetime's worth of sunshine before they are eighteen years old. So kids have to be especially careful.

Be sure to wear a sunscreen with an SPF rating of at least fifteen. Don't use tanning beds. Tanning might look cool now, but wrinkles, elephant skin, and cancer won't look good in a few years.

What about tanning lotions?

A sunless tanner, or tanning lotion, is something you spread on your skin to make you look tan even though you haven't lain out in the sun. Generally, they are safer than lying out in the sun, but that is a decision you'll need to make with your parents. Sometimes it looks nice, sometimes it looks goofy. If you *do* decide to use it, here are some things to remember:

- Buy a product that says it won't turn your skin orange (some of them will no matter what).
- Try it on a test area first to see if you like the color. Wait several hours before making a decision; it can take that long to develop the full color.
- It's best to avoid a sunless tanner on the face unless the product says it's for faces (even then, use it cautiously).
- Use a small craft or makeup sponge to apply it, or put on thin toss-away gloves. Otherwise you'll end up with orange-stained hands that take days to fade.

- Have someone else do your back—be sure to pull your hair up first.
- Don't use a spray—it's too hard to control.

There's another way to have a healthy, year-round top-to-toe glow—having perfectly clean skin! Make sure you bathe or shower at least every other day, and don't use really hot water. It might feel good, but it's drying out your skin. Warm water is best. Be sure to apply lotion to your skin while it's still warm but after you have toweled off. The lotion will absorb better, making your skin glow. Here are some other things to help you. . . .

Cool Tools

- **glycerin soap:** It will help keep your skin smooth.
- **loofah or bath mitt:** Rub it gently against your skin to help shed dead skin cells.
- **sponge on a stick:** Use it to clean your back. Backs and shoulders have a tendency to break out in pimples, so you'll want to make sure you use one of these.

Deep Cleaning

On the nights that you don't shower, just before bed wet a washcloth with warm water, rub a little soap on your washcloth, and close your eyes as you gently wash your face, your neck, and behind your ears. Afterwards, splash-rinse clean and softly pat dry with a clean towel.

Aah. Ever notice how good you feel after you wash? Clean. Fresh. Pretty. Guess what? That's what your heart and spirit need, too.

[Says the Lord,] "No matter how deep the stain of your sins, I can remove it. I can make you as clean as freshly fallen snow."

Isaiah 1:18b

A lotion bar is a solid lotion that you just roll onto the skin. You can find the ingredients at a craft store.

Easy Lotion Bar

You'll need:
- 2 ounces beeswax
- 1 ounce cocoa butter
- 1 ounce almond oil
- fragrance (by the drop, until it is the scent you want)
- deodorant tube

With an adult's help, melt the beeswax and cocoa butter in a glass container in the microwave or in a clean pot on the stove. When it is completely melted, remove from heat and add the almond oil. Then add your fragrance. Pour into the deodorant tube and let it set up completely. Rub all over your body after a shower or a bath. Now you're ready for bed.

Sometimes we do bad things or think wrong thoughts or say something mean. These are some sins. We all sin all the time. After we sin we can feel unlovable or wrong or cranky but not know why. Sin makes us unclean inside. But Jesus says He is willing to forgive us anything—any sin at all! When we sin, we feel bad because we're wrong. And that feeling won't go away until we repent (which means to be sorry for what we've done and turn away from that sin, deciding not to do it again); confess (tell Jesus and others what we've done wrong); and finally, ask for forgiveness, really meaning it from the heart. Each time we do something wrong, we need to ask for forgiveness from anybody we have hurt or done wrong to. We need to ask for God's forgiveness, too. Whenever we do anything wrong, we do it against God. That's something to think about. God says that He will remove our sin and forgive us, because of the sacrifice of Jesus Christ.

> *But if we confess our sins to him, he is faithful and just to forgive us and to cleanse us from every wrong.*
>
> ❈ 1 John 1:9

Make sure you take time each day not only to wash your skin but to ask the Lord to purify your heart, too. Confess your sins to God, asking Him to point out anything you may have forgotten about, and then ask Him to forgive you. He will! Nothing feels so good, so fresh, and so pretty as being truly clean. You'll sleep better, too.

Meet Stephanie . . .
A Girl Like You

Stephanie has Netherton's Syndrome, a rare skin disease. Although she works hard to take care of her skin, her skin cracks, bleeds, and peels. Her hair doesn't grow in all over her head. Has it made her weaker and more embarrassed? Here's her story, in her own words:

What is it like to have a skin disease?

With Netherton's Syndrome, your skin peels all the time—especially on your feet and hands. My skin is usually red and burns most of the time. My hair doesn't grow out—it comes out like bamboo shoots, leaving lots of bald spots. I itch constantly and am in pain. I have had to sit out in the porch in the backyard at eleven at night because I was too itchy to sleep. I've sat crying in the bathtub to make the pain go away.

How do people react to you?

When people see me, they usually stare. I wonder if they think I am ugly or are wondering what is wrong with me. I wish they would ask me questions instead of stare. I like it best when people just treat me normally. I do wish I didn't have this condition, but I also believe that having this has made me a stronger person.

How?

I've learned to like myself for who I am inside. Girls need to look past their looks and look inside. Beauty is a person who is caring, kind to others, and not stuck-up or mean. When I think of all the things people have said about me, and how I deal with this, it makes me proud. That is what makes me feel pretty. Outsides always change, but I would not want to change who I am on the inside, except to grow stronger.

Our skin covers most of our body—it takes the most space, does a lot of work, and takes a lot of care. Keeping it clean, healthy, and protected is a lifelong job. It is durable and strong. And yet, as Stephanie learned, the real strength of a person lies underneath her skin, inside her heart. As you let Christ direct more of your life, and live each day as He would, you grow stronger, like Stephanie, no matter what is happening on the outside. Each day, ask for forgiveness when you need it. No matter what sin has stained you inside (worse than orange-tanned hands), He will make you whiter than snow. Better than skin, Jesus will protect us and hold us together, inside and out.

CHAPTER
3

Face the Facts

But what did he see in the clear stream below?
His own image . . . a graceful and beautiful swan.

—The Ugly Duckling

Your face is almost always the first thing people see when they look at you—it's the center of attention. If you were to take pictures of people and cut them into pieces, mixing them up like a jigsaw puzzle, you could almost always recognize whom the faces belonged to, but not always the other body parts. People remember faces because they connect us to one another.

Looking face-to-face is a way to be close to someone. If you face a friend while she's talking, you grow closer in the conversation. When the Bible tells us to "seek God's face," it is telling us to look for and follow Him and His ways. His "face" is used to represent who He is. Turning your face away from someone is a way to put distance between you, like if you're angry with a friend and turn your back to her. In the Bible God says He has turned His face away from people for a little while because of their sins. Faces are the most personal way to show someone what you feel.

In this chapter you'll learn how to take care of and make the most of your face. It's totally fun and an important part of your look and yourself. Remember, though, for good or for bad, whatever is filling your heart and soul will shine out from your face.

Shape Up

Your unique face, and everyone else's, has a shape. Understanding the shape of your face can help you decide what haircuts might look best on you and—when you're old enough—where to put makeup.

Zits! Help!

Sometimes our faces cause us more problems than we'd like. When we're growing up, that can mean breakouts. You may have noticed the skin on your face is changing. If it isn't now, it will be

Get a big hair band or scarf and pull all of your hair away from your face. Stand in front of a large mirror and see what shape your face is closest to.

oval: Just about any cut looks good with an oval or egg-shaped face. Take your pick!

square: Soften the look with rounded edges—soft, rounded bangs or rounded ends just past your shoulders.

round: Try to make your face look more oval with a style that keeps the hair close to the sides of the face and has more height on top of your head.

diamond: Make your hair fuller and more rounded toward your chin to even out your style.

pear: Focus on making your hair full at the top to balance the fuller, lower part of your face.

heart: A softer, curlier, chin-length look would be perfect.

Remember, face shape is only a place to begin. For example, if you want to draw attention to your nice eyes, have your bangs cut. If you want your face to look longer or your nose to look smaller, pull your hair back from your face.

very soon. It's growing up, too. When you were young, you probably had smooth, clear skin. But as you get older and your hormones kick in, your skin changes, too.

Your facial skin has three layers. When you develop a blemish (otherwise known as a pimple or a zit), it begins in a pore or follicle in a lower layer and erupts—kind of like a volcano—on the top layer.

Chocolate, pizza, and greasy foods do not cause pimples. A few things *can* combine to bring those blemishes on, though:

- oil, which your facial skin is making more of during this time in your life
- bacteria, which are naturally on your face
- dead skin cells, also a normal part of the skin life cycle
- irritation, from harsh soaps, creams, toners, or washing too hard
- stress and/or hormones

Test to see if your skin is oily or not. You'll need:

  two white cotton balls
  rubbing alcohol (ask your mom or dad for help)

Don't wash your face. Dab a little rubbing alcohol on the cotton ball and rub it alongside your nose. Wait for fifteen minutes, and then do the same thing again, on the same side of the nose that you wiped fifteen minutes earlier. If any oil or dirt colors the cotton ball, your skin is on the oily side.

How do I get rid of pimples?

How sensitive your skin is to pimples depends on a lot of things. Some of it is just your age—almost everyone your age will have some zits at some times. Some of it is genetics—a family inheritance. Some of it is how you care for your skin. This is the part you can do something about.

First, don't clean your skin roughly. Use warm water—not hot—and a soft washcloth. The washcloth will help remove dead skin cells. But be sure to stroke gently across your face. If you are too rough—scrubbing, for example—you are not cleaning better; you are irritating your skin. That makes it *more* likely you're going to get pimples, which is just what you don't want!

Use a cleanser or soap that is gentle. One that dries skin out too much will just irritate your face. Don't use masks that have scrubbers in them; that will irritate your skin, too. Be sure to go to bed with clean skin each night.

After washing your face, you can apply an acne treatment cream or gel to the area that is having a break out. An ingredient you want to look for is benzoyl peroxide. Start with the lowest percentage benzoyl peroxide, and if it doesn't help after a couple of weeks, move to a higher percentage. More is not necessarily better. If you use one that is too strong, it will inflame your skin, which will lead to more pimples.

How can I make pimples blend into my face without using a ton of makeup and cover-up?

You can use a lightly tinted benzoyl peroxide solution; some of them are colored to blend in with certain skin tones. Also, if you're not scrubbing your face, it won't get so red and the pimples won't be as noticeable. A light lotion can help soothe the redness.

The best kinds of lotion for girls your age are

- noncomedogenic: does not clog pores
- nonacnegenic: does not irritate pores

Another way to care for your skin is a steam facial. Here are two ways to do it at home!

For either method, first pull your hair back with a headband.

#1

Go into the bathroom and shut the door. Turn the hot water on in the shower and let the room fill with steam. Sit near the shower, but not close enough to get wet.

#2

Have your mom or dad fill a bowl with very hot water. Lean your face over the bowl and drape a towel over your head to trap the steam.

After your face has bathed in the steam for five to ten minutes, gently cleanse your skin, rinsing with cold water (which will close your pores now that they're clean).

Eye Spy

Other parts of your face need special attention, too, like eyes and ears.

Your eyes are, as someone once said, your windows on the world. You will want to take good care of them by

- getting your eyes checked every couple of years. Even if you can see fine, a doctor can make sure your eyes are healthy;
- sitting at least an arm's length away from the computer monitor or television screen when playing computer or video games or watching TV;
- not sharing eye makeup if you wear it.

Take good care of those ears, too. Make sure you don't clean out your ears by sticking a cotton swab in them—it can cause permanent damage to your hearing. So can cranking the music too loud.

I don't like the way I look with glasses. What should I do?

It's a funny thing—girls who have to wear glasses normally don't like how they look in them, while some girls who *don't* wear glasses are dying to wear them.

First off, see if you can get some new frames. Your glasses become a part of your face, and you have to like how they look. There are tons of new styles to choose from. If it's been a while since you had new glasses, maybe your parents will allow you to

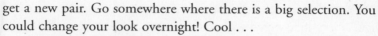

get a new pair. Go somewhere where there is a big selection. You could change your look overnight! Cool . . .

Second, perhaps you're old enough to try contacts. This is a decision that needs to be made with your parents and your eye doctor. Together, you can decide what's best.

Speaking of Contact

No, not contacts, *contact,* as in eye contact. Be sure to look people in the eye when they're talking with you. It's a sign of respect and affection. When you look away from them, it's like saying you'd rather be *anywhere* else than in the room with them. It says you're not listening. You need to listen closely, too. When you listen without interrupting, you tell the person you value her thoughts.

Eyes and Ears

We don't often consider our eyes and ears as gifts, but think of what life would be without them! Be sure to thank God for them next time you watch a lacy snowfall or groove to your favorite tunes. A thankful heart is a beautiful heart.

Ears to hear and eyes to see—both are gifts from the Lord.

Proverbs 20:12

Here's a thought:

What does beauty look like to a blind person?

Express Yourself

Did you know there are actors called mimes who never speak a word during their entire performance? Instead, they use only actions and expressions. Their most important tool is their face, which is usually covered with white makeup. Mimes can show almost any emotion and expression so clearly that everyone in the audience knows if they are joyous, angry, or surprised.

Your face shows a lot about you, too. People around you can see what you're feeling by the look on your face. Do you walk through the day with a frown or worry lines? Or do you show peace, love, and joy? Faces send messages. What message is yours sending today?

A glad heart makes a happy face.

❀ Proverbs 15:13a

Mimes aren't the only ones who wear makeup. Some girls and women do, too.

Do you really need makeup to look beautiful? Wouldn't God have made us with makeup on if He wanted us to look that way?

Wearing makeup is a personal choice. Some people choose not to wear makeup, while others enjoy it. Some people wear makeup on some days and none on others.

Of course, you don't need makeup to be beautiful, but wearing makeup isn't wrong, either. God did make us, but He also left us with lots of freedom and choices.

The main thing to remember if you choose to wear makeup:

Wear some that is subtle—that is, it's soft and not too easy to see. It should highlight what you have, not cover it up or make a big deal of it.

Lots of makeup contains ingredients from fish! An ingredient called pearl essence (or pearlescence) is the silvery stuff found in fish scales that's used to make some lipstick, blush, and eye shadow sparkle.

All my friends wear makeup to school, but I can't yet, not even mascara. What should I do?

Don't be in a hurry. Most women try their best to look like they're not wearing *any* makeup! You can make the most of your natural beauty. If your parents don't allow you to wear makeup, they are making a choice in your best interest. Be thankful for the love and protection they provide! Wearing makeup does not make you mature or pretty. It might be fun, but your real prettiness glows from the inside out.

If you really want to try something, you might ask your mom

if you could rub a little petroleum jelly into your eyelashes for shine, or even just a quick brush of clear gloss across your lips.

How do I get my skin to have a pretty glow?

There are a couple of ways to do this, but the healthiest—and easiest—is to get enough exercise. When you exercise, your blood circulates, and that brings the rosy color to your cheeks. Also, a little sweat will free up the grime trapped on your skin, helping your skin to glow after you clean it off. Right after cleaning, put a light coat of lotion on your face and you'll seal in the glow.

Makeup artists tell women that their blush color should match the color of their cheeks right after exercise. You can get the same look by running up and down the stairs a couple of times—and it will be completely natural!

There's an even better way to light up your face, to make it lovely to look at. Yep, you guessed it—it comes from inside. . . .

Wisdom lights up a person's face, softening its hardness.
Ecclesiastes 8:1b

Meet Maya . . .
A Girl Like You

Maya is a popular children's theater actress in Seattle. She started acting when she was little, at the Seattle Children's Theatre Drama School, and is still at it! Maya uses her clothes as part of her character, but as an actress, she relies on her face as one of her most important features to express what's happening inside each character.

How did you get started acting? What plays have you been in?

I did a theater summer camp and enjoyed it so much that I was determined to audition for something. On my first audition, for *Children of Eden*, I got the part! I kept going. Soon, I was participating in the wonderful Seattle Children's Theatre (SCT) summer stage program. This led to working with the SCT main stage, and then to more things. I've also been in *Rags*, *Sound of Music*, *Time Again in Oz*, and *Gypsy*.

What is the best part about being an actress?

I love acting and the attention and adrenaline rush. That is why I would like to become an actor. However, it is a hard job, and I am not sure if I want to do it for a living. The worst parts of acting are being told you are not the best or that you are not talented, especially if you are an understudy and you have to see your "competition." A hardship for adults is low wages. But being told you are great is the best!

Actresses wear makeup and use their faces as part of their character. How does that work?

My mom or I usually apply my makeup. It depends how big the theater is to know how much to put on. Usually I put on base, blush, eye shadow, eyeliner, mascara, and lipstick. It is a stronger kind of makeup than you wear for other purposes. It is to make you show up with the lights.

Little "bits" are important in getting across the whole story. That means I have to use my eyes and my eyebrows and my smile and my expression to tell the truth of what is going on inside each character. My expressions and actions tell the story, too.

Does pretending to be someone else for a while change how you think about yourself? How?

Sometimes the character wears off on me. I can't help it when I start living the character for a while. But really, I want to stay myself. It is nice to learn from a character's mistakes. I think being someone else temporarily has made me more myself.

As Maya says, faces tell what is really happening inside. This isn't true for just actresses doing characters; it's true for you and me, too! Our faces are windows into our hearts.

We say people's faces "light up with joy," but we never say their arms do, do we? When we say someone "looks troubled," we mean the look on her face is sad and bothered.

The world does have troubles that can bring us down, harden us from the inside out. But the Lord says to cheer up; He has overcome this world. As you grow closer to the Lord and live the way He designed you to—full of grace, faith, humor, and love—you become wiser, and that makes your face soft and lovely to look at. Because of Him, we can begin each day fresh again, our faces lit with joy.

CHAPTER 4

Tress Distress

Rapunzel, Rapunzel, let down your hair!
—Rapunzel

Hair is often the first thing we notice about someone when we first meet them. Is it brown or black or blond or red or a twist of two of the above? How many of you have grown out your bangs (I'm raising my hand) only to get it cut into layers again, dissatisfied with the final look? The phrase "bad hair day" has become a part of our vocabulary, and we use it to describe anyone who might be crabby. Why? Because too much of our mood depends on what our hair looks like.

As much as we notice someone's hair before they speak or act, once they say or do something, our interest is drawn to that instead. Hair holds our attention for a few minutes. Acts of kindness, words spoken gently to soothe a hurting heart—those remain forever. Next time you're brushing some shine into your hair, take time to plan words and actions that will bring attention to the One you serve.

What Is Hair?

Hair that is already out of your scalp is actually dead fiber. It is alive when it is under your skin, and then it is pushed out of the follicle like toothpaste through a tube. Once it's out, it's not alive anymore. But it still needs to be cared for in order to look nice. You can even care for your hair from the inside!

You Are What You Eat

Or rather, your *hair* is what you eat. Healthy hair is built inside a healthy body—and that means lots of water, good protein, and fruits and vegetables are important for nice hair. Crash dieting and eating too little or not enough high-quality food can actually cause your hair to fall out!

Lots of sleep time means good health for your hair. Another good reason to get to bed on time tonight!

You're All Wet

How often should you wash your hair? That depends on if it is dry or oily, sweaty or clean. Most people think washing your hair every other day is just fine, unless you're involved in a sport every day or your hair is more oily than dry. You can use any kind of shampoo you like; more expensive does *not* mean better quality. Don't forget—never brush wet hair; instead, comb through it with a wide-toothed comb or a pick. Wet hair is fragile, and brushing can make it break off.

Two ingredients often found in shampoos are *sodium laureth sulfate* and *sodium lauryl sulfate*. The first one, with *laureth* as a middle name, is milder and gentler on your hair. The second one, with *lauryl* as a middle name, works, too, but it is stronger—it's also used to strip axle grease off of cars!

Mmmmmassage

After washing, or even before, treat your scalp to something wonderful—a massage!

Underneath your scalp skin is a thin layer of muscle—so treat yourself to a head massage whenever you wash your hair. Get the hair wet, put a small amount of shampoo on your palm, and then rub your palms together. Spread the shampoo over your hair and massage it into your scalp. It will not only clean the scalp and relax the muscle, but it'll feel really good, too!

Cool Tools

Now that your head and scalp are in good shape, use gentle tools on them, too.

- **pick or wide-toothed comb**
- **brush:** Choose one with rounded bristles and a cushiony rubber backing; or for smooth, straight hair, use one with natural bristles.
- **blow dryer:** One with low settings is best, so you don't damage your hair.
- **curling iron:** If you must. Go easy—it can singe, burn, or dry out hair.
- **soft, spongy rollers:** They're better for your hair than a curling iron. Roll up after a shower and wake up with curly, bouncy hair. The wider the roller, the wider the curl, so you may have to experiment with roller size.
- **slick plastic or wrapped hair bands:** *Never* use rubber bands for ponytails and braids. They will break hair every time. Remember, it can take a year to grow six inches of hair, and you could break it off with one use of a rubber band.
- **barrettes**
- **ribbons, bows**

How do I get my hair shiny?

Part of the shininess is genetic, meaning it comes from your mom and dad. Healthy hair will shine more than unhealthy hair, fine hair more than coarse hair. You might try using a product with silicone in it. Just rub a little bit on your hands and smooth it on after drying. Brush through gently. Don't use too much, or you'll get greasy-looking hair.

Time on Hair = Time in Prayer

How much time each day do you spend on your hair? We all want hair that looks lovely, that shines, that is attractive to ourselves and to others. But what really makes us attractive? The most important shine we have is the light we shine into the world—that attracts others to the One who is in us, Jesus Christ.

> **Let your good deeds shine out for all to see,**
> **so that everyone will praise**
> **your heavenly Father.**
> Matthew 5:16

Tune in to Him through prayer to know what good deeds to do. Here's a simple equation: **time on hair = time in prayer.** If you spend ten minutes a day brushing, styling, or checking on your hair, be sure you spend ten minutes a day praising, talking with, and spending time with God. It doesn't have to be all at once—five minutes twice a day is good, too. You can start a prayer notebook—write down your prayer requests, and then when it is answered write down the date and how it was answered. When you're feeling blue, you can look back over them and gain faith and courage. You'll be someone whose inner beauty lights up everything around you, and that's the beauty that counts!

Remember, healthy hair comes from a healthy body. Once it's out of the scalp, though, you can condition it to keep it in good, smooth shape. Buy a gentle conditioner to partner with your shampoo, and for extra-special care, mix up a special treat for your tresses.

Tropical Conditioner

You'll need:
> 1 avocado (peeled and mashed)
> light coconut milk

Combine the mashed avocado with some coconut milk. Mash together until it's smooth and about as thick as shampoo. Comb it through the hair and let it sit for ten to fifteen minutes. Wash out.

When you're ready for bed each night, tie long hair back into a ponytail. That way, when you toss and turn at night, your hair won't tangle. It'll be a smoother brush-through with fewer broken hairs in the morning.

Brittle? Coarse? Rough?

No, not your hair, your attitude. Just as brittle hair is rough to the touch, a bristly attitude is hard on the heart. How do you soften up? Spend time reading your Bible. Just as good nutrition on the inside is necessary for healthy hair, good spiritual nutrition is necessary for a healthy heart.

Get a good, easy-to-understand version of the Bible and read it through, a couple of verses or even a chapter each day. A good place for a Christian to start is reading through one or two of the Gospels, like Matthew or John. Read about Jesus' life and hear His actual words. Get to know the One you desire to follow. After you finish the book, you'll be amazed at how close you feel to God.

If you like, you can follow along with what your school, Sunday school, or church is studying. If you have a memory verse, read the whole chapter that verse is drawn from. Romans 12:2 tells us to be changed from within by a new way of thinking, and 2 Timothy 3:16 tells us that the Bible is the tool to use for that. Soon your heart will be softened, your attitude will be looking up, and you'll have the unmistakable beauty that comes from a changed life.

A strand of healthy hair is as strong as a strand of copper wire.

- **Don't** pull hair back too tightly in a ponytail, braids, or barrettes. You can damage the scalp to the point where your hair might fall out.
- **Do** use loose braids, gently clipped barrettes, and soft ponytails.

How to French Braid

You can start with wet, damp, or dry hair. Just make sure your hair is free of knots. Start by combing your hair backward as if you want to put it into a ponytail. Take a section at the top of your head as high up as you would like the braid to start. Split the section into three strands and begin to braid your hair as you normally would. The only difference for a French braid is that you take hair from the outside and add it to the three inside strands as you braid. For example, before you begin to braid the left strand over the middle strand, take a thin section of hair from the upper left side and add it to the left strand.

Continue to add sections of hair from both sides as you braid down your head. It helps to do this in front of a mirror. If you run out of side hair, continue with a simple braid until you reach the end.

How to Make a Bun

First, gather your hair and pull it back. Use a hairbrush to bring your hair up into a ponytail at the top part of the back of your head. If you want a lower bun, start with a lower ponytail. Use a covered elastic hair band to hold the ponytail in place. The tidier the ponytail, the better the bun. Twist the ponytail and coil it into a tight circle. Secure the bun to the rest of the hair with hairpins by sliding each pin through the outer part of the coil and then into the base of the bun.

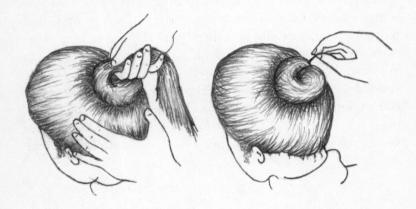

All Dried Up!

What's the best way to dry your hair? Blot it with a towel as soon as you come out of the tub or shower (be sure not to twist the hair or wring it in the towel; it can damage the hair). Then, after running a wide-toothed comb through it, let it dry naturally. If you blow dry it, use a cool or warm (not hot) setting and let it dry naturally for a few minutes before you begin.

I wish my hair were thicker. What can I do?

Whether your hair is thick or thin is determined before you are born, according to your mom and dad's background. The hair width is determined by the size of the follicle it comes through—the wider the follicle, the thicker the hair. The shape of the follicle determines hair shape—curly, waved, or straight—also before you are born. If your hair is thin, don't despair. You can find shampoos and styles that will make it look lovely. Look for ones that say "thickening" on the label. Blow dry your hair to add fullness, or braid it wet and then take the braids out after it's dry. Remember, no one has hair exactly like yours, so you have something unique and beautiful. Ask a stylist and make the most of it!

If you are African-American, your hair still needs the same gentle treatment and healthy feeding as other girls' hair, but because of the follicle and hair shape, it has some special concerns. Be sure to wash mostly the scalp and not scrub the hair too hard—the shape of African hair makes it difficult for the scalp oils to reach the end of the hair, so it can dry out more quickly. If you choose to wear your hair in braids, be careful to have someone experienced do the braids, and remove or rebraid them every six weeks to protect your hair and scalp.

Something Smells Good!

Shampoos with some of these scents will get you in just the right mood:

- **Lavender** helps you relax.
- **Rosemary** energizes you.
- **Rose** smells fresh.
- **Mint** wakes you up.

The Bible tells us that one of Jesus' followers, Mary, poured expensive and sweet-smelling oil over Jesus' feet and then dried them with her hair. For her to dry them with her long hair was a sign that she put her worship and respectful treatment of Jesus ahead of her personal beauty and concern over what others would think about her. Are you embarrassed to follow Jesus in front of others, or do you know His opinion is the one that counts the most?

Then Mary took a twelve-ounce jar of expensive perfume made from essence of nard, and she anointed Jesus' feet with it and wiped his feet with her hair. And the house was filled with fragrance.

❁ John 12:3

I have split ends. What should I do?

Once a hair is split, there is nothing that can make it go back together. If you have lots of split ends, you might get it cut to a shorter style. If you don't want to cut it, or if the split ends are all over, you can use a conditioner. The conditioner won't make the hair go back together, but it will keep it smooth, which will make it *look* like the split ends are gone. Remember, healthy bodies and gentle care will avoid split ends.

Here are some other common problems:

- **Dandruff:** Dandruff is the little white flakes from your scalp that peel off and can get in your hair or on your clothes. Most of the time it's actually from stress! So try to relax and turn your worries over to God. You can also use a mild dandruff shampoo, or even a good conditioner if a dry scalp is the cause.
- **Bad Hair Cut:** Don't you hate it when this happens? Try parting it on the other side or down the middle. Try wearing it clipped back, or if it's summer, wear a baseball cap. And remember, it *will* grow out, probably faster than you think.
- **Dull Hair:** Try a gentle conditioner, or use a natural lemon hair spritzer to give it a little shine. But be careful. Over time, this can cause hair to lighten slightly or dry out.

Mix in a bottle and spray on hair:

> juice of one lemon
> 12 ounces purified water

How many hairs does each person have?

Each person has up to 150,000 hairs on the head—isn't that amazing? Jesus tells us that God knows just how many we each have. He doesn't tell us that to prove how much God knows (though He knows everything); Jesus tells us that so we won't be afraid and so that you will know how very much he cares about every detail of your life.

> *Not even a sparrow, worth only half a penny, can fall to the ground without your Father knowing it. And the very hairs on your head are all numbered. So don't be afraid; you are more valuable to him than a whole flock of sparrows.*

❀ Matthew 10:29–31

Meet Amy . . .
A Girl Like You

Amy recently donated her hair to Locks of Love, which provides hairpieces to kids suffering from long-term medical hair loss.

Why did you decide to donate your hair to Locks of Love?

I donated my hair to Locks of Love because I wanted my hair cut shorter and wanted to help someone else who needed it. My friend had donated her hair a few years ago, and I thought it was a cool idea to help kids who have lost their hair because of medicine or from their sickness. Also, I didn't know how many kids like me with red hair would donate, and I wanted kids who had lost red hair to be able to have their same color again. Red hair rules!

How much time did it take to grow your hair long enough for them to use?

Well, it was already pretty long when I decided I wanted to have it cut short. Once I decided that, my mom braided and measured my hair to see how long it was. In a couple of months, I had enough to cut some off and still leave enough for a cute haircut! I could hardly wait to put my braid in the envelope we had ready and send it to Locks of Love. A few weeks later, they sent me a pink post-card saying they had gotten it in the mail and thanking me.

It feels really good to know I'm helping someone else!

Do you think your hair makes you pretty?

My hair is a part of who I am, like part of my personality. I feel kind of different with short hair than I did when my hair was longer, even though I'm still me. I think most of how pretty I am comes from the inside, because Jesus is in my heart. But I also like to look pretty on the outside, too. I feel as good about myself with short hair as I did with long hair because I know my true friends know I'm still the same on the inside.

I'm sure if I had no hair at all I might be afraid to go out around lots of people and do the normal things that I like to do—like play sports or go shopping. I guess that it's more than just giving some of my hair to someone. It's like giving her something that can make her whole life a little better, or make her feel special again.

Just like Amy does, it's okay to love your beautiful hair and take good care of it. What made Amy especially beautiful, though, was her kind gift of her hair to someone less fortunate. Have fun with your hair—doing it differently and cutting it and braiding it and making it sparkle. Just remember that your words and deeds—what shines before others to bring them nearer to you and nearer to God—are what will last.

For information on donating hair, please contact *www.locksoflove.com* or call (888) 896–1588.

CHAPTER
5

Say Cheese!

*Who gathers up little teeth and
leaves a treat in their place?*

—Legend of the Tooth Fairy

We use our mouths to eat and drink. Our mouths share our words, our laughter, and our cries. Our lips kiss good-night. We even share our feelings without talking through smiles and frowns. One of the most important things we do with our mouths is thank and glorify the One who gave it to us! David said,

No wonder my heart is filled with joy and my mouth shouts his praises!

❀ Psalm 16:9

Besides praising God, you can use your mouth to lift people up or to tear them down with the things you say. Each morning as you brush your teeth, commit to God—and to yourself—to use your mouth only to encourage and never to tear down.

You had only twenty baby teeth, but you will have thirty-two adult teeth when they are all in. The baby teeth "clear the path" for many of the adult teeth so they come in at the right places.

Drinking milk is important for healthy teeth and bones because it gives them the calcium they need. If you eat too many sweet things, the sugar will coat your teeth like tar.

Morning Breath

Be sure to brush your teeth every day and also floss once a day. There are more than one hundred kinds of bacteria living in your mouth (really!)—and those bacteria cause morning breath.

Cool Tools

After brushing, try red plaque-disclosing tablets. Chew one up after brushing your teeth, swish it around in your mouth for about thirty seconds, then spit and rinse out your mouth. Now look in the mirror. Every place that has a red patch on your teeth still has unbrushed plaque on it—just dying to eat a hole into your tooth! Your parents can buy red plaque-disclosing tablets over the Internet or ask your pharmacy or dentist.

Change your toothbrush at least four times a year. Otherwise, you're brushing with old, dirty bristles. One good way to remember is to change your toothbrush each time the season changes—on the first day of winter, spring, summer, and fall.

Want something cool to do with all those old toothbrushes? Make bracelets out of them. If your brush is a groovy color or shape, the bracelet will be even better.

Get an adult to help you with this. First, pull all of the bristles off of an old brush with a pair of pliers. Then start a small pan of water boiling. Set the toothbrush in the water, and when the plastic is warm, have an adult pull it out with some tongs and twist it into a bracelet shape. When it cools, slip it over your wrist and start a new trend.

Clean and Fresh

Clean applies not only to your teeth, but also to your words. Are you tempted to curse? Tell bad jokes? Say nasty things about people who bug you? Don't.

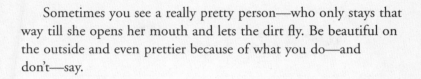
Sometimes you see a really pretty person—who only stays that way till she opens her mouth and lets the dirt fly. Be beautiful on the outside and even prettier because of what you do—and don't—say.

> **Do not let any unwholesome talk come out of your mouths, but only what is helpful for building others up according to their needs, that it may benefit those who listen.**
>
> Ephesians 4:29 (NIV)

Chewing Gums

Without your gums, your teeth couldn't chew. Be sure to brush your gums and your tongue whenever you brush your teeth. Not only will you keep your teeth longer, but you'll also avoid bad breath. Puffy gums and stinky breath aren't anyone's idea of beauty.

Be sure to floss. If you only brush and don't floss, you miss up to thirty percent of the places you need to clean. Have you tried flavored dental floss? Grape and mint are especially tasty. Flossing helps keep the goop out from between your teeth, which not only is gross to look at but also makes your mouth smell bad. Yep, more bad breath. *P.U.*

Cool Tools

Buy a mini tin of breath mints and keep it in your lunch box so you can have a mint after you eat lunch. If you eat hot lunch, keep some mints in your locker and in your backpack. You just never know when someone special will come up and say, "Hi!"

For pictures, does it look better to smile with your teeth showing or not?

There isn't really any one best way; it depends on how you feel about how you look. Try standing in front of a mirror—in private—and smile in a lot of different ways, some with your teeth showing, some without. You will soon find what looks best to you. Then, next time you have pictures taken, just use the smile you chose in advance. One wise mother advises that the best smile comes from laughing. Laugh aloud and see how pretty you look!

You might like how you look with your teeth showing but don't like your teeth. In that case, you could wait till all of your adult teeth grow in, wait till your braces come off, or try some tooth-whitening toothpaste. You don't have to keep one look your whole life!

In Japan it is considered rude to smile with your teeth showing. That's why a lot of Japanese girls hold their hands over their mouths when they laugh.

Do tooth whiteners really work?

Yes. Most bleachy tooth whiteners aren't recommended for kids, though, because they have strong chemicals in them. You have to remember, every person's teeth start out a different shade. Toothpastes that say "whitening" are different from bleaches and strips, though, and are generally safe for kids. Ask your dentist, or try this safe method for tooth whitening at home:

Sprinkle a little baking soda on your toothbrush before adding toothpaste. (You only need a pea-sized amount of toothpaste, by the way.) Brush teeth as usual. This will help remove stains and brighten teeth.

Metal Mouth

Sooner or later, most of us have braces. If you're one who didn't need them—congratulations to you! If you're wearing some now, or will be soon—congratulations to you, too. Your mouth is getting prettier and healthier. Be sure to clean between the braces—check in a mirror to make sure there's no food stuck in there after lunch.

What colors of rubber bands for braces are the coolest to have?

Since you have to wear braces, you might as well look at them as a fashion statement. A lot of girls coordinate their band colors with their favorite clothes, or they make up club colors that they and their metal-mouthed friends all wear together. Maybe you'll all wear blue or wear your school colors during basketball season or wear red and green in December. No one color is the coolest, but it's cool to make a plan and show it off!

Motor Mouth

Metal mouths can be pretty, but motor mouths aren't. It's no fun to be around someone who has to talk all the time—and never listens to what anyone else has to say. Make sure you're someone who listens more than you talk. Not only will it make you a better friend, it will help you be wise.

> *So let your words be few . . . being a fool makes you a blabber-mouth.*
>
> ❊ Ecclesiastes 5:2b–3b

The same holds true when you're angry. Sometimes people say things that are so hurtful you want to fling it back at them right away. Instead, close your mouth and think it over. You may see things differently the next day, and even if not, you will have set

an example for speaking with self-control, a truly beautiful thing.

Don't sin by letting anger gain control over you. Think about it overnight and remain silent.

Psalm 4:4

Ouch!

Smiling can be painful—if your lips are cracked, that is. Cracked lips usually come during cold weather or when you've been outside a lot. Flaky lips don't look too hot, either. Sometimes you get cracked lips if you've been sick or if you're not drinking enough water. Be sure to drink enough water, and wear a lip balm or a lip gloss all the time during the winter months. Since some do have medicines in them, don't use the ones that say "medicated" for too long. Use a smooth, non-waxy one, or the moisture can't set in. Try to buy one with sunscreen in it; you'll be protecting your pretty smile for years to come.

Double Ouch

What hurts worse than cracked lips? Gossip. Almost nothing hurts worse than people talking about you—when what they are saying is mean. If anyone has ever gossiped about you, I'll bet you felt like David when he wrote this:

They visit me as if they are my friends, but all the while they gather gossip, and when they leave, they spread it everywhere.

Psalm 41:6

Everyone is tempted to gossip, but gossip isn't pretty. In fact, it's downright ugly. For girls who want to be beautiful inside and out, gossip has to go. Next time you're tempted, keep your lips zipped. And when someone is gossiping around you, tell them, "I don't want to talk about it," and change the subject. It's not only good for your inner beauty; it will save your friendships. The Bible says that gossip separates the best of friends.

May the words of my mouth and the thoughts of my heart be pleasing to you, O Lord, my rock and my redeemer.

Psalm 19:14

Meet Julia . . .
A Girl Like You

Julia is a regular girl who wanted to
help kids who were having a hard time. She also wanted a
project she could do with her friends and her mom. Was
she successful? Read all about SendaChildaSmile.com, in
Julia's own words. . . .

How does SendaChildaSmile.com work?

Some children around the United States are upset with
their lives, and we pack envelopes full of stuff that will
make them happier. Friends and relatives of the children
send emails or letters recommending that we send a smile.
They pass the information on to us, and we send the envelopes of stuff to make them feel better.

What do you and your friends actually do to help?

We stuff the envelopes. First we get the list of names.
Then each of us stuffs the envelope with something special,
like a special letter to them, stickers, a craft, and other
things. Then we decorate the envelopes and mail them. We
have several families get together, have pizza, and stuff
envelopes. It usually takes us two to three hours.

My mom read about it and we talked about this being
something we all could do together. It makes me feel good
because I have a good life, but it also makes me feel bad
because I wish that the kids I'm stuffing envelopes for had a
better life.

What kinds of trouble are the kids having—the ones that you are packing smile boxes for?

Some have cancer, some are unhappy with their lives, some are treated poorly by their parents, and some are really sick or their brothers or sisters or parents are really sick.

It makes me feel sad that they are having problems. It makes me feel like Thanksgiving is all year long for people like me. I hope that they will feel better about their lives because they know that people care about them. I do.

How does this make you feel as a Christian?

It makes me feel like I'm doing what the Lord has told me to do. I'm taught in church and at home how to give and help others. I would tell other girls to go for it, find a way to help out other people somehow! Smile! Do what you believe in. I would tell them to talk to their parents and friends and make a plan. Their reward would be feeling good that they did something right.

It makes me feel better about myself. I think that it makes the kids we send the envelopes to feel like smiling, too. I think they are feeling that, even with their situation, they are loved. When I get mail, I feel important. I think they feel important when they get mail, too.

I would tell other girls to get involved. It's fun, you're helping other people, and it's what God wants you to do!

What kinds of words will bring a smile to those around

you? Each day, ask God to open your eyes to someone who needs a smile. You can give an honest compliment or a soft word of encouragement when someone makes a mistake; you can invite someone who needs a friend to hang out, or tell a parent or a teacher how much you appreciate them. Jesus says the words of our mouths flow out of what's in our hearts. When you are growing more beautiful inside, it flows out of your mouth, showing love to everyone around you. Like David, we want our words to be pleasing to God. Each day, use your mouth to bring a smile to at least one person in your life. Watch how it brightens the faces around you, which will only brighten your own face and deepen your real beauty inside.

You can nominate someone to receive one of these envelopes at *www.sendachildasmile.com*.

CHAPTER 6

Ten Plus Ten

*Heralds traveled throughout all the kingdom,
declaring to all that the Prince would marry the lady
whose foot fit the slipper that he had picked up.*

—Cinderella

When God designed us, He gave us amazing sets of tools to use. We have eyes to see and ears to hear, of course, and we can use them to look and listen to others. Our hands and feet, though, are our primary tools of serving others. It begins in the heart—a heart to serve others, to do good to and for them. Once we have determined to serve, the opportunities are endless. How can your hands serve others? How can you use your feet to help people in need? Let's learn about and take care of these tools—and then set them on the path to serve.

Amazing

Your hands and feet—including ten fingers plus ten toes—are amazing. When you add up all of the bones in your hands and feet, it totals nearly half the bones in your whole body! Because of this (and their many muscles), your hands and feet have incredible flexibility, strength, and ability to make exact movements.

To see how important thumbs are, try picking up a fork and knife and then eating without using your thumbs. Hard, isn't it?

I would like to have really soft hands. I have tried lots of different lotions, but they don't work. Any suggestions?

Yes! Our hands say a lot about us. We use them to talk, touch, love and hold, and work. Because people spend time looking at our hands and because we touch others with them, we want them to be clean, neat, and soft.

First, make sure you keep your hands clean. You need to wash them often—after you go to the bathroom, of course, and before you prepare food. Also wash them after you've been outside playing, or before doing any work with your hands. When you have a cold, be sure to wash them often so you don't transfer germs to other people. One good way to make sure you're washing long enough is to rub the soap between your fingers and palms as you say the "ABC's" quickly in your mind. When you reach Z, rinse off. Put lotion on them after baths and before bed and rub the lotion in well.

Up to twenty-five hundred left-handed people die each year from using products made for right-handed people!

Two I-Promise-They-Work
Mother/Daughter Hand Softening Treatments

#1

You'll need:

1 pound paraffin wax (you can buy this at a hardware or craft store; it's easy to find)

glass bowl

Chop up the paraffin and put the chunks into the bowl. Microwave on medium until the wax is melted. Stir the wax and let it cool so that it's warm, not hot. Smear it all over your hands. Let it dry completely, about ten minutes. Then peel the wax off, letting it fall back into the glass bowl. Store the leftover wax—you can use it many times. Rub lotion into your hands afterward.

#2

You'll need:

2 cups oatmeal

4 tablespoons honey

4 tablespoons water

Blend the oatmeal in your food processor or blender till it's almost powder. Mix it with the honey and the water. Rub it into the back of your mom's hands, and then let her rub it into your hands. Let a thick layer dry on each hand. Rinse off with warm water and apply lotion.

Tools

Even more important than how your hands look is what they do. As we discovered above, our hands might be our most important tools. Pretty hands are hands that do work that have eternal value.

Her hands are busy spinning thread, her fingers twisting fiber. She extends a helping hand to the poor and opens her arms to the needy.

❀ Proverbs 31:19–20

What those hands were doing were useful things for the family, things for others' well-being. Those hands reached for the poor and the needy.

Choices

What can you do to serve with your hands? Can you clean up the kitchen, sweep, vacuum, and pick up the family room without being asked? Will you use your hands to do the jobs nobody wants, like cleaning the bathroom? Can you hug your sister or give a friend a high five or a handshake of encouragement? Can you help your teacher or assist a friend with her work? Rake leaves for a single mom on your street?

Your hands can, of course, help the poor, meaning those who have no money. Maybe you can use your hands to do some extra work around the house and donate any money you earn to missions. Sometimes, though, people around you have simpler needs. A new girl may need a hand extended in friendship. A teacher might need a handwritten note of encouragement and thanks. A disappointed brother might need a hug. Your hands were meant for work: What kind of work are you choosing for them to do?

Don't forget to do good and to share what you have with those in need, for such sacrifices are very pleasing to God.

Hebrews 13:16

I bite my nails, and they are really ugly. I tried willpower, and nothing seems to work. Help!

First of all, you have to realize why you are biting your nails. Nail biting is a nervous habit—that means it's something you do when you feel worried or stressed. You might not even realize that you're doing it. First, every time you catch yourself biting your nails, ask yourself, "What am I feeling upset about right now?" Usually it will be something that just happened, that you were just thinking about, or that you are worried might happen.

Next, take really good care of what nails you have. Give yourself a manicure, and paint them a pretty color. Once your nails look good, you won't want to bite them as much. Buy some awesome polish as a reward for not biting your nails—and remember that biting nails with any polish on them can harm you. Also, you'll feel better inside when you figure out what's upsetting you and solve that problem instead of biting your nails.

Here's how to do a great manicure:

1. Remove all old nail polish.
2. File your nails with a soft nail file. File gently in one direction only, toward the middle of the nail, shaping into an oval. Don't overdo it!
3. Soak your hands in warm soapy water. After the skin is softened . . .
4. Use a cuticle pusher to gently push your cuticles back.
5. Finally, dry hands and nails. Lotion your hands and apply clear or colored polish if you want.

Make sure you keep your nails clean regularly even if you don't manicure. Wash them each day, and use a nail cleaner tool (with your mother's permission) to scrape away gunk underneath your nails.

Cool Tools

Did you know that you can use regular acrylic paints, like those you use for hobbies, to paint your nails? This makes it possible for you to make many more designs. First, paint on a clear base coat, and be sure to put a topcoat of clear on after the paint designs dry. You can buy the paint at a craft or drugstore and dip a toothpick into the paint to paint on your small shapes. You can make groovy designs like these:

- Paint your nail pink and use yellow and green acrylic paints to make flowers.
- Create holiday nails with a heart, shamrock, or flag.
- Share your faith—paint a gold cross, a Christian fish, or WWJD on each nail.
- Celebrate the seasons with a snowflake, sun, beach ball, or pumpkin.
- Paint your initials on one finger and friends' initials on the others.

White Out

If you don't like painted nails—or don't have time to take care of them—buy yourself a whitening stick at the pharmacy. After your manicure, rub the stick under your nails to make them clean and white. Apply clear polish and you'll have beautiful hands.

Fingernails grow nearly four times faster than toenails!

Get Walking

Speaking of toes and toenails, if your hands are your most important tools, your feet motor you from here to there. It's fun to pick out cute shoes—pick some that showcase your personal style. Take good care of your feet, and they'll be pretty no matter if they're wearing skinny little sandals or the chunkiest boots.

DO

- Wear shoes that fit. Don't wear shoes that you've outgrown because you love them, or buy some too big because you want to wear them a long time. Shoes that don't fit can cause blisters, corns, or ingrown toenails, which are unhealthy and painful! Wobbling on pinched feet or slogging around in too-big shoes is definitely not beautiful!
- Wash and polish shoes when they get scratched up or dirty. It doesn't matter how nice your clothes look if your shoes look like a mess.
- Cut your toenails straight across, not curved in, or you might get nail and toe infections.
- Take off your socks as soon as they are damp. It's easier to get blisters with moist socks. And don't sleep with socks on—feet need to breathe, too!

Butterflies taste with their feet!

Beautiful Feet

Your feet will take you wherever you want them to go. Where does Jesus want your feet to go? He told us to go and make disciples. Who do you know that needs the Good News—a neighbor, your piano teacher, a classmate, your grandparents? Pray and ask the Lord with whom He would like you to share His good news, and then don't be afraid to point your feet toward that person and spend more time with him or her in love. Let your feet be beautiful by using them to take you to share His good news here on earth, and that will be beautiful in heaven, too.

> *But how can they call on him to save them unless they believe in him? And how can they believe in him if they have never heard about him? And how can they hear about him unless someone tells them? And how will anyone go and tell them without being sent? That is what the Scriptures mean when they say, "How beautiful are the feet of those who bring good news!"*
>
> ❀ Romans 10:14–15

What can I do when my feet are hot and sweaty inside my shoes? They stink and it's embarrassing.

Your feet sweat for the same reasons the rest of you does: being hot and being nervous. Your feet have thousands of sweat glands between them, and some people can sweat up to a cup a day through their feet! You can help by keeping your feet clean and making sure they are dry when you put your shoes and socks on. Wear cotton socks if possible. If you like, you can sprinkle some baby powder into your socks—it will help keep your feet dry and smell pretty, too!

Those feet do a lot of work. The American Podiatric Medical Association says the average person takes 8,000 to 10,000 steps a day—or several miles. It all adds up to about 115,000 miles in a lifetime—more than four times around the globe.

Kiss a Frog If You Want To

It won't give you warts. According to the American Academy of Dermatology, warts are noncancerous skin growths caused by a viral infection in the top layer of the skin. Warts are passed from person to person. You don't even have to touch the person or her wart; just touching something she has touched or walking barefoot on the same floor can be enough.

The time from the first contact to the time the warts have grown large enough to be seen is often several months. The risk of catching hand, foot, or flat warts from another person is small.

Some people get warts depending on how often they are exposed to the virus. Wart viruses occur more easily if the skin has been damaged in some way, which is why people who bite their nails or pick at hangnails get more warts. Some people are just more likely to catch the wart virus than others, just as some people catch colds very easily.

You can treat warts with medicine your parents buy at the drugstore, or your doctor can take them off. Normally it doesn't hurt. Be sure to keep the area clean while you're treating the warts.

Foot Wash

Jesus used His hands to do the lowliest of jobs—a job some of his friends seemed embarrassed for Him to do: wash their feet. Washing feet was the job the lowliest servant did. It required them to kneel at the feet in a servant's position, down on the ground—complete humility. Because people wore sandals in those days, the dirt would be ground into their feet. I'll bet they didn't look too good or smell too good. When Jesus washed the feet of those who were His disciples, He showed us that in His kingdom, there is nothing embarrassing about serving others, no matter what the job requires. In fact, He commands us to serve one another in the lowliest ways, too. Don't rush past these questions till you answer them: Whom are you serving this week? How is God asking you to serve someone in humility?

> *After washing their feet, he put on his robe again and sat down and asked, "Do you understand what I was doing? You call me 'Teacher' and 'Lord,' and you are right, because it is true. And since I, the Lord and Teacher, have washed your feet, you ought to wash each other's feet. I have given you an example to follow. Do as I have done to you."*

> ❀ John 13:12–15

Meet Elizabeth . . .
A Girl Like You

Although Elizabeth likes to use her hands for her own enjoyment—playing the piano, for example—she also saves time to use her hands and sewing skills to help make quilts for Quilts for Kids. Quilts for Kids gives the quilts to kids who are in unsafe situations at home.

What do you do?

My mom doesn't sew, so I work on these projects with my mom's friend. First, we pick out the fabric. We always pick out the best colors and patterns, ones that I would like for myself. Then we cut the fabric into cool shapes. I sew the pieces together, and when I am done, my mom's friend quilts them.

We write cards telling the kids who are going to get the quilts that we care for them and want to send this gift, even though we have never met them. It goes to some people who meet with families in trouble. These people give the quilts to the kids in those families.

I use my hands to quilt for the kids and to write caring notes, too.

Why did you decide to do this?

I learned what *merciful* meant at school—being tender-hearted toward someone or helping them feel better. I decided I wanted to do this. Some people call quilts "comforters," and I hope that these will comfort kids in bad situations. I think the kids feel really sad. They can take the quilt with them if they have to leave their homes to go live someplace else. The quilt can be theirs forever.

How do you feel when you do this?

Sometimes I feel like an angel must feel—you know, helping other people for God. I think Jesus would be telling me, "Good job," because most of the time I use my hands to do stuff for myself and not for other kids. I feel really bad that they need help, so I want to help them. I think any kid could do this or something else to help someone who has a need.

Jesus asks us to do for others as He did for us. Sometimes we take pleasure in the way we use our hands and feet to serve—by sewing, for example, or caring for a neighbor's child if you like kids. Sometimes, though, it might be unloading the dishwasher (my least favorite chore) or folding laundry when we'd rather be reading or talking on the phone. Sometimes we'd rather use our feet to bike with a friend when God wants us to use them to walk to a new girl's house and show her Christ's love. Beautiful hands and feet are hands and feet that serve, as He tells us to do. And when we obey Him, the reward is from Him, too, which is peace and love and joy—beauty from the inside out.

If you're interested in helping kids the way Elizabeth has, check with your local police department to see if they have a program like Quilts for Kids.

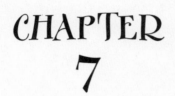

CHAPTER 7

Nothing to Wear

Once there was an emperor whose only thoughts were about dressing in beautiful clothes. He changed clothes often and loved to show off.

—The Emperor's New Clothes

O ur choice of clothes tells a lot about us—whether they are bright or soft, clean or dirty, modest or not. Because we wear clothes every day, it can be great fun to look your best. You can make pretty choices and look good! Each day, besides deciding what clothes we are to wear, we choose what kind of attitude to put on for the day. Yep, it's a choice! You can wear an attitude of discontent, walking around with a frown and slumped shoulders. You can wear an attitude of anger, with your head pulled back and arms crossed, a look that says, "Don't talk to me." Or you can put on love, warming your smile and your heart to those around you from the first bowl of cereal to the final nightly prayer. When you pick out your clothes, pick out your attitude, too!

Rainbow

So—how to go about choosing your clothes? Some colors look great on you and blah on your friend, while some might wash you out but look terrific on her. How can you tell which clothes colors look best on you? Try this handy quiz to get a head start.

Do you have blond hair and light skin (the skin that doesn't tan but burns easily)? Some of your best colors will be:

light blue gray	deep rose	orchid
rose beige	rose pink	soft fuchsia
cocoa	burgundy	watermelon
periwinkle blue	rose brown	powder pink
medium blue	blue red	sky blue
light lemon	raspberry	soft white instead of
yellow	plum	pure white

Do you have blond hair and golden skin (the skin that tans well and doesn't burn easily)? Try these colors:

camel	orange red	coral pink
light clear gold	yellow green	bright red
golden tan	emerald	salmon
golden brown	turquoise	violet
peach	warm beige	ivory instead of pure
apricot	navy blue	white
light orange	light blue	

Do you have red hair or warm brown and reddish brown hair with golden skin? These colors will look good on you:

warm beige	terra cotta	purple
camel	salmon	forest green
yellow gold	orange red	tomato red
gold	turquoise	jade green
pumpkin	coffee brown	oyster instead of pure
orange	teal blue	white

Do you have dark brown hair with either pale or dark skin? Try these colors:

taupe	chinese blue	royal blue
light true gray	pine green	navy
true blue	shocking pink	charcoal gray
lemon yellow	true red	pure white is the best
true green	royal purple	white
hot turquoise	blue red	

What if you already have some clothes that aren't in your best colors? You can still make them work—maybe with a T-shirt or jewelry in one of your best colors. Or wear your best colors close to your face, mixing and matching pieces. Some girls choose to wear mostly one shade at once in order to appear taller.

Your personality may also play an important role in what color to wear. Sometimes a more romantic girl will choose the lightest color in the appropriate palette, while a dramatic, outgoing girl will wear the most intense colors. But sometimes the colors you choose may let something inside out. A quiet girl may choose to wear red as a way to express a bolder side of her, while a more outgoing girl may choose to wear something muted as a way to express her softer side.

How do I wear clothes that look nice and are in style without always having to wear what everyone else is wearing?

It is important to learn very early that personal style and origin-ality are the reasons why people notice us, not how much our clothes cost. Pay attention to what you are wearing when people compliment you. If more than one person notices what you are wearing, it means that you are doing something right.

You don't have to wear what everyone else is wearing. Wear what suits *you*! And don't worry about having to have the best or most expensive. God knows you care about how you look and will provide for your every need. Pray and ask for His guidance. He cares about everything *you* care about—even your clothes!

> *Look at the lilies and how they grow. They don't work or make their clothing, yet Solomon in all his glory was not dressed as beau-tifully as they are. And if God cares so wonderfully for flowers that*

are here today and gone tomorrow, won't he more surely care for you?

❀ Matthew 6:28b–30a

For almost one thousand years it was considered fashionable for Chinese women to bind their toes underneath their feet till their toes rotted and died! Millions of women endured this fashion, which kept their feet from growing longer than four inches, ever. The practice was made illegal more than fifty years ago.

Build a Team

If you buy clothes that work well together, you can have more outfits for less money. Make sure you buy pants and shorts that will go with several different shirts. Even dressy clothes should be able to go with shoes you can wear with a couple of different outfits. You can give each outfit a separate look with the accessories you choose—jewelry, hair wear, etc.

It's also important to get clothes that are the right size. If they are too tight, they won't be modest or attractive. Too big and you'll be swimming in materials!

A skirt is not too tight if you can move it all around your hips without unzipping it but you can still feel the pressure of the fabric. It is too large if you do not feel the fabric at all.

A top is the right size if you can comfortably cross your arms in front of your chest; but if you can't even feel the fabric on your back when you cross your arms in front of you, it is too large. If it gaps or clings to your skin anywhere other than your arms, it's too small.

Speaking of Modesty . . .

Modesty is important for all Christians—girls and boys, women and men. Modesty has two meanings: First, being modest means not having too high an opinion of yourself and not being conceited or too proud of how you look. We choose to be modest by what we choose to wear or say or how we act. We don't call too much attention to ourselves.

The attitude, of course, begins and grows in the heart.

Modesty also means choosing to wear suitable clothes. It means *decent*. It means choosing to wear clothing that doesn't come close to showing private areas and isn't see-through or too tight, and wearing appropriate undergarments. What modesty means in your family is a good topic to discuss with your mom.

Modesty isn't only for our regular clothes. Bathing suits and even pajamas should be modest, too. You are God's *treasure*. Treat yourself and your body with respect.

> *They should wear decent and appropriate clothing and not draw attention to themselves by the way they fix their hair or by wearing gold or pearls or expensive clothes.*

❀ 1 Timothy 2:9

Make Your Own Sleepover Nightshirts

You'll need:
    puffy paint
    extra-large sleep shirts in any color

Next time you have a sleepover, buy a sleep shirt for every girl who comes. Use the puffy paint to doodle, sign everyone's name to everyone else's T-shirt, and put the date on them. Each time you go to bed after that, you'll remember a cool night with your buds.

For hundreds of years women used huge iron plates or whalebone undergarments to make their waists fashionably small. Many times these things caused a woman to be unable to breathe well or even cracked her ribs!

All That Glitters

Jewelry is a fun part of your wardrobe, too. You can wear costume jewelry or real jewelry and change it every day! Just like with clothes, though, the purpose of jewelry is to add to and enhance what you have, not call attention to itself. If you wear jewelry that is expensive just to show off or call attention to yourself, that would be immodest. If you wear jewelry that quietly blends in with and enhances what you are wearing or has special meaning to you, that is the right way to add a special little touch.

Why does some gold jewelry turn my skin green?

This is a common problem. It is simply a chemical reaction between you and the metal and may happen sometimes. Most jewelry is not pure—it is made of some sort of alloy. *Alloy* means that the jewelry is not pure gold.

Twelve karat gold means the jewelry is fifty percent alloy and fifty percent fine gold.

Fourteen karat gold is forty-two percent alloy and fifty-eight percent fine gold.

Eighteen karat gold is twenty-five percent alloy and seventy-five percent fine gold.

Sterling silver has approximately 7.5 percent alloy added to

92.5 percent silver. Silver can also cause harmless skin staining, usually black or green.

Clean Your Jewelry

Mix a teaspoon of dishwashing liquid into a cup of water. Put the jewelry into it. Use a soft cloth or an old soft toothbrush on the jewelry. Dry off with a soft cloth.

If you have silver, you can do the same thing, using a little nub of silver polish instead of the dish soap.

Be careful with "fake" jewelry. Sometimes pieces can chip off during cleaning.

Laura Ingalls Wilder's wedding ring featured not diamonds but garnets and pearls.

Birthstones

Do you know what your birthstone is? Check out this list:

January—garnet
February—amethyst
March—aquamarine
April—diamond
May—emerald
June—pearl
July—ruby
August—peridot
September—sapphire
October—opal
November—topaz
December—blue topaz

And the most important piece of clothing you must wear is love.

Colossians 3:14a

Meet Davina . . .
A Girl Like You

Davina works with her family to send donated clothes to poor children in Moldova. Moldova is a very poor country in Eastern Europe. Before they received the boxes from Davina's church, most of the kids never got new clothes—they had few clothes and only shoes with holes in them, even in the dead of winter. Now, though, the kids get nicer clothes, and Davina, for one, is happy about it. Here's her story, in her own words. . . .

What do you actually do to get clothes to poor people?

We tell people at our church what we are doing, and we have boxes at our church to collect the clothes. Once a month, I am in the church basement looking over the clothes people bring in. I make sure there are no stains or holes in the clothes. Then I put them neatly into a box that will go to Moldova. Most of the time it takes three to four hours to pack these boxes.

What first gave your family the idea? How does being involved with this make you feel?

Our church was helping Moldova, and the people who did this job stepped down. God led us right to it. This job makes me feel good because I know I am helping kids who don't have the kinds of things that I have. They don't have the stuff that I do, and they don't experience the wonderful things that I do. Anyone could do this at her own church.

How does your work with collecting clothes for the Moldovans change the way you feel about clothes?

Like other girls, I am excited when I get new things. Now, though, I think of other people who don't have this stuff. In fact, they don't have anything. It makes me think what I wear doesn't have to be perfect. I am just glad to have clean, fitting clothes to wear, and to give good clothes to these other kids, too.

Have you heard any personal stories about kids who have received the clothing?

The kids who get the clothes know it is from people who care about them. One thing I hear a lot is that no matter what it is that we send, they always love it. It changes how I feel as a Christian, because I know God is giving good things to these wonderful boys and girls. And they are happy with whatever they get.

What would you say to other kids who might want to do something like this?

I would tell them, let God direct you to a job that He has for you, like He did for my family. We wanted to help, and we saw some ministry that needed someone to work in it, so that's how He led us right to it! God will show you the way. If other kids started volunteering, I would tell them it is hard work, but when you are finished you are proud of yourself because you know you have done something special for someone else. You don't earn money;

you earn love from other kids and people.

It also helps me realize I can wear what is me and not just what is cool. It's okay to be different. I would tell girls they would really enjoy this job and it will change their lives.

When you were a little girl, your mom or dad chose your clothes for you each day. You had no say in the matter, and you probably didn't care much, either! But now you are growing into a young lady, and you have choices. Every morning, ask yourself if what you're wearing says what you want it to say about you. Mix clothes and jewelry to express yourself. You can be clean, neat, and modest and still have your own unique sense of style. Decide each day what attitude you're going to put on. You're old enough to choose that for yourself now, too! You may not get a lot of outward comments ("Hey, that attitude looks great!"), but the beauty inside will shine through, and people will want to be around you. That kind of appreciation may be quiet, but it may also be the most welcome.

CHAPTER
8

Mind Your Manners

"If you would only spare my life, I would be sure to repay your kindness." The Lion laughed and let the Mouse go. Shortly after this the Lion was caught by some hunters, who tied him up with ropes. The Mouse, recognizing his roar, kept his promise and came and gnawed the rope with his teeth to set the Lion free.

—The Lion and the Mouse

Manners are really the result of a wonderful recipe: Mix together kindness, respect, thankfulness, and self-control, and you will have beautiful manners, which will serve you wherever you go. When you have nice manners, people want to be near you, and you will like and respect yourself.

> *Since God chose you to be the holy people whom he loves, you must clothe yourselves with tenderhearted mercy, kindness, humility, gentleness and patience. You must make allowance for each other's faults and forgive the person who offends you. Remember, the Lord forgave you, so you must forgive others.*
>
> ❀ Colossians 3:12–13

Isn't it wonderful to be a holy person whom God loves? It's wonderful that we can share His love simply by the way we treat others. Are there any of the above five ingredients (mercy, kindness, humility, gentleness, and patience) missing from your manners? Pray for them and add them to your daily interactions. The most important part of good manners is thinking of others before yourself. Whose feelings can you take into consideration today?

Hello—Good-bye

Our first chance to show our nice manners is when we greet someone. Looking people in the eye tells them that they count. Saying hello and asking how they are shows that you care. Be sure to say good-bye politely, too. If it's someone you don't know well, it's always nice to extend your hand to say both hello and good-bye. If you know them, a hug lets them know how much you care.

Even when you greet someone you see often, like your parents, siblings, teachers, and friends, say hello and good-bye with a smile.

It makes all the difference for a "sunny" day.

Handshaking as a greeting started when people wanted to make sure that the person they were meeting didn't have a weapon in his right hand!

Home Sweet Home

Well, it stays sweet if we help it to. Good manners at home means caring for and respecting the people and things around you. Pick up your stuff; take care of it. Talk to your parents as you would like your friends to talk to them—no sassing, but lots of respect. Isn't it funny how we sometimes treat our friends' moms and dads with more respect than our own parents?

Honor your father and mother.

✿ Exodus 20:12a

Be sure to use your most respectful manners in speaking with other adults, too. Address them as Mr. or Mrs. unless you've been told to call them something else. Wait till they are done talking before asking questions, and always ask if there is something you can help with.

Something to think about:

"Pretty is as pretty does."
—Ma Ingalls

Party Time!

Whether you're going to a party or throwing one yourself, manners matter! One of the best rules to go by for all manners is to ask yourself: "How would I feel if this happened to me?" Do for others as you would like them to do for you.

Simple rules for a good time had by all:

- Don't hand out invitations or talk about a party at school unless everyone is invited.
- Don't invite some kids to a party and only a few or one of them to stay overnight afterward—how would you feel if you had been "banished" from the party?
- If you are invited to a party, call the hostess as soon as you know if you can attend to let her know.
- Pay more attention to the girl who is having the party than to anyone else—even if your best friend is there, too!
- When you leave a party, thank both the hostess and her parents.

Thank You!

Young ladies make sure that their thank-yous are written out. Someone has taken a long time to think about (and pay for) whatever gifts you receive. Make sure you send a written thank-you note to the giver. Proper thank-you notes include mention of the item and how it will be used. Thank-you notes don't have to be long at all. In fact, you can send a small card. You should send them within two weeks of receiving the gift.

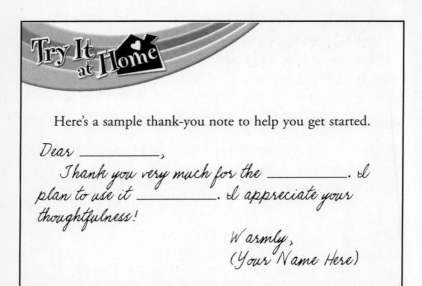

Try It at Home

Here's a sample thank-you note to help you get started.

Dear _____,
    Thank you very much for the _____. I plan to use it _____. I appreciate your thoughtfulness!

                                    Warmly,
                                    (Your Name Here)

Did You Know?

A guest in Japan is given small candies and cakes, which are served on pieces of paper. To be polite, he must wrap the food he cannot finish in the paper and carry it away with him.

How come some friends just do the talking all the time? I like it when my friends listen to what I want to say, too.

People have a lot of different reasons for "hogging the spotlight." Sometimes they want people to know how smart they are. Sometimes they think they are the only ones with something important to say. Mostly, though, people just get excited and caught up in whatever they are talking about and don't think about the fact that they might be talking too much. If it's a good friend, you might take her aside and tell her she's so great at conversation, but it's harder for you, and would she mind helping by giving you a chance to talk more often? If it's someone you don't know well, you might just choose to spend time with other friends. When her audience starts to disappear she'll get the message.

Don't be selfish; don't live to make a good impression on others. Be humble, thinking of others as better than yourself. Don't think only about your own affairs, but be interested in others, too, and what they are doing.

Philippians 2:3–4

At the Table

Putting all of the silverware, glassware, and china in the right places is a sign that some occasions deserve formal treatment. But even when the table isn't set fancy, your table manners should be in top shape. Here are some important things to remember:

- Don't talk with food in your mouth. I know you know it, but we all still do it sometimes.
- If you don't like something that is served to you at a friend's home, just leave it on your plate without comment, or if you serve yourself, choose other items instead. Be sure to thank your friend's parents for the meal, no matter what.
- Don't gnaw on your food. Cut a piece small enough to chew properly and place it into your mouth. Chew with your mouth closed till you swallow.
- It's polite to put your fork and knife down in between each bite.

Have a fancy dinner party for you and three friends to practice your manners. Send out beautiful, formal invitations. Ask everyone to dress up. You and your parents can choose a fancy menu and cook most of it up in advance. Maybe your dad or mom could be the waiter! Set the table correctly, and serve decaf coffee or herbal tea with cream and sugar afterward.

In the United States, the knife is held in the right hand and the fork in the left. After the food is cut, the knife is put down and the fork is transferred to the right hand. In most European countries the fork remains in the left hand.

The Golden Rule

The Bible says that everything the laws and prophets teach can be summarized with one short sentence. It's your guide for life.

Do for others what you would like them to do for you.

❊ Matthew 7:12a

Meet Morgan ...
A Girl Like You

Morgan attends Final Touch Finishing School, which simply holds etiquette classes for all kids.

What is finishing school?

Finishing school is fun; you go to learn manners and the right way to do things. It changes how you feel about yourself and how you present yourself to others. It teaches you to shake hands properly, how to answer the phone, and how to properly set the table.

I just started to take classes, and I want to learn more. I want to learn more so I will be proper and have better manners. It teaches you to present yourself in a proper way. When you feel like you are proper, then you feel more self-confident.

How did it change you?

By going to etiquette class, I learned to have better manners and feel more confident about myself in different situations. I learned to shake hands with people and make eye contact. I learned how to sit and stand properly from a chair, how to answer the phone and take messages, how to set the table, how to eat a candy bar without making a mess, and to remember to listen to people and let them talk.

Manners are also about being clean in appearance—

clean hair, nice nails (no chipped nail polish), deodorant, brushed teeth, etc. I learned how to stand in front of an audience or class and present yourself or introduce people to the audience class and where to place a name tag on your clothing. I learned how never to separate the salt and pepper at a table and to treat other people's property with respect. I never knew all of this stuff before!

Does having nice manners change how people interact with you? Does it change how you feel about other people?

Yes, because I have learned that people like to be treated nice. I really can control my actions around them. People like it when you have nice manners and can handle your behavior.

I also learned that kids who have nice manners don't talk back to their parents. They say please and thank you. Now I am more aware of my actions and how I treat other people. I am more respectful to my siblings, other adults, and property.

What do you think manners say about a person when she is a Christian?

It shows that I really care and respect people, as Jesus would want me to.

As Morgan said, the most important part of manners is caring for and respecting other people. Sometimes this means not doing what you want to do (letting someone else go first), or doing something you wish you didn't have to (writing out all those thank-you notes.) If you pay attention to others and are interested in what they are doing, you are treating them well. Treating others well is a simple and yet very touching way to share God's love and radiate that love from the inside out.

Dear Lovely Young Ladies,

You are the future! Your charming selves will grow and develop with more loveliness as the years increase and you stay clean inside and out. Your beauty is an individually wonderful gift from your Creator, and you shine with His glory! You are awesome and beautiful, and I'm here cheering for you to be the best that you can be!

**Your beauty should come from within you—
the beauty of a gentle and quiet spirit.
This beauty will never disappear, and
it is worth very much to God.**
1 Peter 3:4

With love,

Sandra Byrd

Acknowledgments

I got lots of ideas in lots of places. And lots of it I already knew! Some people generously gave me permission to reprint information. They are:

American Academy of Dermatology
Marisa@theimageconsultant.com
PageWise, Inc.
Pioneer Thinking
Salonweb.com
Shan-Yee Poon Ballet School, San Francisco
Soap Crafters Company
Vermont Soapworks

The original creator of reprinted material was sought in every case. If you have questions, please write to the address below.

Some of my references come from books and Web sites with content that should be previewed by parents or grandparents first. So if you are a parent or grandparent and want additional references, please send me a note requesting such at the following address:

Sandra Byrd
P.O. Box 1207
Maple Valley, WA 98038

Fun and Friends!

THE HIDDEN DIARY contains stories you won't want to put down. Two new friends have found an antique diary whose pages will lead them on countless adventures and mysteries. As they grow, come along for the fun with:

1. *Cross My Heart*
2. *Make a Wish*
3. *Just Between Friends*
4. *Take a Bow*
5. *Pass It On*
6. *Change of Heart*
7. *Take a Chance*
8. *One Plus One*

◆ BETHANYHOUSE